**Anything we touch
with love —
will be better.**

*To Esther Helen Nesseth Rusten,
of whose life, this book
is an extension.*

TABLE OF CONTENTS
    PREFACE – 4
    THROUGH HARD TIMES – 9
    COME, WALK WITH ME – 17
    IN THE DELIGHTFUL – 27
    JUST OVER THE RIDGE – 37
    A PATH ONCE TAKEN – 51
    ALONG A LONELY STRETCH – 59
    TOUCH OF WATER RUNNING – 69
    A LEAF-STREWN PATH – 79
    THE YELLOW TUFTS OF SUMMER – 91

*Text and photographs Copyright ®
1987 by Philip Rusten*

Journeys of the Heart

*To Tom —
Happy Anniversary —
And Best Wishes —
Phil Rusten*

Text and Photographs

by

Philip Rusten

*Lithographed in Canada by
The Bryant Press Limited
Toronto, Ontario*

Preface

This life of mine, that began in the hearts and bodies of my parents, now more than ever seems an extension of theirs. My dreams, my heart—wishes, are my own, but I recognize in myself the same life force, the same hoping, the same determination, I saw in the parenting struggle of those who gave me birth . . . and more. It is this journey of the heart I now walk for them as I do for myself and for those I love and care about here and now.

The most significant journey we ever take is the one "of the heart". We travel along a path dimensioned by our dreams and our admirations. Our yearnings cut the home-ties, choose our companions, delineate our life's work. Our loves, our heart-aches, our deepest convictions lay out the course our life will take. Without a dream . . . without desire . . . we go nowhere. We remain immobile, energy-less, a captive of an empty heart.

From my parents, I also learned the love of work . . . the sweat, the struggle, the slow tedium of progress. Aspiration without work achieves nothing. Work nourishes life, makes possible the reality of any dream, and, more importantly, work brings integrity to the self. To work is to be in harmony with the creative forces of the universe. Idleness is but the spaces between the joys of achievement.

At the core of our being we live a time-machine existence, traveling through memories and aspirations with equal ease. The present shackles us to reality only until we can break its bonds by the yearnings of our heart. We are the happiest, and perhaps the healthiest, when our dreams are the most vital.

→

So, it is no casual thing to pen these words, for the dream knows no end. It is a journey—not a destination. Process, alone, has value. The tree grows because that is what is does best—first up, then out—until all the options are played out. Then, from its collected self, another tree is born . . . and another . . . and another . . . and another. And life goes on . . .

More than ever, my perspective now is fashioned by idealism. It is the healthiest way to live, and no risk is greater than that which bids us settle for the least. Idealism fuels even the most tired moments, and, like oxygen, clears and cleanses the mind, energizing when nothing else will.

Now it is a conscious decision—an act of will—not an unconscious product of youthful energy. And so, *Journeys of the Heart* reflects not only on roads traveled, but on roads leading over the horizon as well. To us all . . . Bon Voyage!

The way we see the world
makes us
who we are.

Spring Meadow

*It takes silence
to penetrate
mystery.*

Morning Light

*A bit of beauty
is a window
in the smog
of dailyness.*

Queen Anne's in Railroad Yard

*Only our thoughts
 keep us
 from being a waste
 of Creation's time.*

Through Hard Times

Winter Willow

The Red Barn

The Snow Storm

That late Fall, my father and I spent our days harvesting a meager corn crop. Amidst corn too short for mechanical pickers to harvest, we walked row by row, day by day, alongside a three-box wagon pulled by our team of horses and, ear by ear, saved what we could. Grueling, unrewarding work characterized those particular years, obviating any tendency to complain or despair. Our survival depended on this work, and we took pride in our courage and dependability.

   On The morning of November 11th, the rain began quietly shortly after we reached the field. It grew with intensity, turning first to sleet, then to driving snow. As the storms's intensity increased, so did the impossibility of continuing. By 11:00 o'clock we had unhooked the wagon and stabled the horses. By nightfall we were snowbound and would remain so for fifteen days. On the 14th day, a community effort enabled on car to get to Brookings for the depleted supplies we all needed. In the interim, we survived. →

This period seems a lifetime of specialized activity more heroic and special than other winters, like a life within a life—more noble than other times. A monotony of measurement occupied us. How many days of the storm, how deep the snow, how much wood do we have, when will we run out of flour—or the livestock out of feed . . . and on it went.

The first stage of the storm covered five days, piling up monstrous snow drifts around the buildings and over the roads and tree lots. Then the winds began with a new intensity as the temperature dropped. Shoveling snow became impossible and unnecessary. We cut steps in the drifts outside the house and walked up and over the tops of them to the barn and the woodlot. By the end of the sixth or seventh day, I could ride horseback over them to visit the neighbors or check on the livestock.

When the sun broke out in the cold crisp air, the South Dakota State Conservation Department issued an emergency call over the radio for help in saving the pheasant population. At night, and when storms came, the pheasants would seek shelter in the grasses along fence rows or in low lying swamp areas where tall dense grass offered warmth and shelter. Now they were covered by a blanket of several feet of snow topped by an impenetrable crust of ice and snow. Though warm enough, they could not get out to forage for food. So we were urged to go the areas where pheasants were known to seek shelter and to break the crust on the snow to release these imprisoned birds.

At seventeen, this appeared to me to be an unusually real emergency, and so for the next several days, along with others, I stomped the marshes, the woodlots, the fencerows and the fields of unharvested sweet clover. Exhausting and exhilarating, the effort saved most of the birds. Like playing a huge punch-card game, we second-guessed the birds and laughed excitedly with each explosion of snow and feather that signaled the release of a healthy, hungry pheasant.

Not all made it, however, and with the passing of days, more and →

more snow-filled frozen bodies surfaced as the snow patterns changed.

   Empathy takes many strange forms. With those pheasants that survived, with the farm animals, with the neighbors and with all living things there emerged a common bond forged by the storm. Even the storm itself entered into this bond for it was as much an alive part of our lives as food or breathing. We came to know its pulse, its rhythm, its power and endurance. You respect things of integrity and strength and this storm was all of that.

   One of the milestones on my journey to manhood occurred on the third day of the storm. The experience, as much as anything, showed me my limits and my worth.

   In the woodlot south of the house, I had a sow and four eight-week-old piglets under my care. They were part of my →

Winter Farm

Oak in Winter

*Adventure
 is simply
 risk overlooked.*

beginning as an independent farmer—my future, as it were. As the storm began, I carried water and grain to "tide them over" for a day or two until the storm abated. It didn't and their need for food for body heat and nourishment grew more critical. Their small shelter was soon almost drifted shut. Unless I could get them out, they would perish.

So the journey began. On by one I carried the fifty pound piglets into the face of the driving snow to the safety of the barn 600 yards away. How many times I fell or despaired in the blinding snow I no longer can remember. One vivid vignette remains. On my third trip, still south of the house, only a third of the way to the barn, I stopped—struggling piglet in arms—and considered giving up. No reserve of strength or will remained. Then the thought of this and the remaining piglet's fate took me over the threshold of despair and I simply went—step by struggling step—the rest of that journey and the next. Three days later I was able to bring food to the sow.

Integrity is being who you say you are, and at seventeen, taken to my inner limits by this storm, I was able to feel both the growth and the reality of being who I said I was—a dependable caretaker of my responsibilities.

There were joyous elements, too, in the storm. Our snowboundness continued in one degree or another for three months. We fed the stock, cut wood, prepared meals and played chess. In this, my first year out of High School, my father and I got to know each other—on either end of a crosscut saw and on either side of the chess board. My mother's meals were never so much appreciated or enjoyed. Warmth radiated for the cookstove, the space heater and from the family. That this winter could generate so much joy in our lives is a wonder in itself. Truly a storm without parallel. We not only survived, we prospered.

Old Oak in the Field

*In the process of realization,
every dream
looks like work.*

Mill Creek Winter

The person
   who forges ahead,
     charts a lonely course.

Come, Walk With Me . . .

Come, Walk With Me. . .

Making Our Way

There is no path through here. I know that. Only the desire to get beyond this jumble of juniper and hawthorne suggests there is one. The mind leap-frogs to the beyond, surmounting the body's frailness.

The desire dims with the difficulty and so does the possibility of a path. Deer go through here. Think like a deer. Twist, turn, go under, around, possibly over. There must be a way. Isn't there always—a way—if we want it enough?

Then in the midst of it, the thorns enlarge, branches become more tangled, openings close in front and to the side. Directions convert to non-directions. The only horizon lies behind. The only known way, the way just travelled. Go back. Don't gamble. It will only become worse. The unkown multiplies, growing stronger than knowledge.

Thus we live. The week before graduation . . . the eve of the wedding . . . the day of retirement . . . all the milestones and the non-milestones. We proverbalize the dilemma—"The night is always the darkest before the dawn. . . ."

Describing doesn't make it easier. Desolation is desolation however defined. That others have known or now experience the same, only slightly comforts. When alone, the path remains just as tangled, the way out just as forlorn.

Then desire becomes stronger than fear. With a combination of reckless abandon and careful decision, a way is made. Beyond the imposing juniper/hawthorne wall emerges a slender opening and beyond that a way that leads to other ways and to a clearing—grassy, sunny, restful. Now the choice is "which way?", not "Is there a way?". Opportunities multiply, halting the journey →

until they are unravelled by a decision. Now easier, now clearly defined, all other choices forgotten, it is possible to follow "the right path".

Thus we live. There isn't a "way". Only desire, determination, courage, intelligence can make one. We share no hereditary imprint with the mud-daubber wasp, who without help, lives, creates, dies. Without a clear path, we face a jumble of thorns, obstructions, a maze of unseen paths and uncut paths. We dream, and desire. We stumble, falter, waver, reach out and go.

It's not much, but it is all we have. It usually is enough.

The Individualist

Oak Creek Canyon

*The participant knows
what the observer
only guesses to be true.*

Things Free

For days now, my mind has turned repeatedly to one single concept for protection and support. The idea is so simple that I didn't know I knew it until in a conversation it emerged clearly and distinctly—like an axiom long believed.

Simply stated, it is this: That which nourishes and supports our real self—our inner being—is always free. No one can ever sell them to us. Only those things needed for the outer self can be sold: clothes, food, tools, decoration. Integrity, confidence, personality, skill, devotion, courage, faith, poise, determination, good-humor, self-worth, understanding, insight . . . all are products of the self and they are free! Circumstance can hinder or help our achievement of any of these, but it is our own inner processes that make them a reality.

We like to excuse our failures by describing the circumstances in which they occurred. Yet in the same circumstance at other times, we surmounted the difficulty and achieved success. No, it is our own effort and decision that makes us what we are.

Yes, we can be so emotionally and intellectually impoverished as to need a boost from another to get us started. But even this depends on our own effort and it cannot be sold to us.

How nice to know that advertisements are irrelevant! I can safely ignore gleaming teeth, chic apparel, sterling electronic marvels, fast powerful machines, without incurring irreparable harm to my personal success as a human being.

How nice to know that real people and real personal power can exist in spite of corrupt bureaucracy, and shallow materialistic social programs. Form does not determine substance . . . and only substance can make us healthy and content.

What deters us from pursuing this idea more often is the difficulty of working on the abstract. Objective things are so much easier to see and achieve. I want to write, so a new word processor will make it possible. A new, softer chair will turn me into a writer—especially if it is in the right, romantic setting. Ah yes . . . the fantasies of things are omnipresent! I've chased so many of them, trying →

valiantly to ignore the cry of the inner voice: "To write, you must write . . ." That is too simple—too technologically barren. Perhaps that word processor would make it faster . . . and after all, isn't it speed that produces quality? "To write, you must write . . ." What a bothersome idea . . . how impossible to ignore.

The simple and the profound are so often identical. Complexity, more synonymous with confusion, is dispelled by the truth. "To write, you must write . . ." Simple. True.

All of this unraveling of thought is occurring in the sterile environment of a hotel room. There are no library books, no easy chairs, no personal mementoes or grandiose window vistas. Every item around me is pragmatic to the ultimate. Whatever inspires or motivates me, I have brought into the room inside myself. The one contribution of the setting is isolation. How fortunate for me that I like the voice of my own thoughts—not exactly an overnight achievement.

Perhaps I underestimate the influence of the row of stately fir trees beyond the motel room window, and for that I apologize to them. It is raining softly, steadily, on their branches and the trees sway gently under the burden of the gathering moisture and the slow moving wind currents the rain has generated. Their stately manner does affect me and I try to be more poised, more accepting, when I look at them. They obscure anything beyond, as well, and that obscurity is no small contribution. Like window draperies, they keep my work within manageable limits.

Whatever, it is a simple environment within which I write these words . . . and it is simple words I write. Yet how powerful they are for me! I know something now that will never disappear. I am stronger . . . more powerful . . . less threatened, than I was an hour and a half ago—all because of an idea that came gliding to rest into my consciousness one late afternoon earlier this week. I wonder, should I mark it on the calendar . . . or will there be another?

Saginaw Forest

The Night

It is night now. The cedars and the oaks stand profiled against the night sky. Puffs of snow on branches and leaves project an eirie white against the evening blues and blacks. Silence blankets all this and me. So unacquainted am I with silence, it is both wondrous and frightening. Every move is a contradiction. Be at rest, the night says. Whisper, look, but do not scurry about.

The night is made for careful movement. It doesn't allow undue bravado, careless posturings of superiority. Approach it carefully, for the night tells the truth about people and things.

Daytime noises, work-day dissonances, the jangle of inner struggles—all echo more loudly as the night envelopes me in private thoughts. Slowly, in the night-time stillness, even these diminish.

Then with muted voices, the night composes its symphony of restoration—sounds played on a lower register—soothing, gentling, restoring.

The mantle of work drops away. Gone, the clocks, the schedules, the date-books. Time is measured on another scale. Slowly it happens. My self gathers up into itself. A calmness comes. I am alone . . . and resting.

First Snowfall

Weeping Cherry

Times taken
  to enjoy
    are the birdsongs
    of our lives.

In the Delightful

Cuyahoga Sunrise

April Sun

The April sun is making indoor work difficult. Momentary samplings of its seductive warmth only intensify the difficulty. What I am doing so pales in importance that rationalization becomes stronger—my will to work, weaker. Tomorrow might be cloudy—possibly even rain. . . .

If this be not wisdom, then it is surely delight. Such pleasure as the warming rays of the spring sun can hardly produce regret. Gratefulness for the stolen moments is a more likely memory.

Buffy, has long since found the sun-spots. Her canine world, devoid as it is from stress, permits pure enjoyment more readily than mine. But I will have it, however delayed it might be. Measuring the time left in the sun's day, and spurred by sun-drenched fantasies more seductive than reality, I work more intensely for the end of this. Temptation to settle for the fantasies almost overshadows the desire for the real. Then it is truly wisdom that shortens the work, opening up spaces for the sun. Fabricating "what might be" cannot possibly create the full life. No matter what our dreams, "real living" must occur.

So I seek the sun. It flows over me, saturating the fabric across my shoulders and arms, storing up warmth for colder hours. There is a flash of memory and I'm back in my childhood on the cellar door south of the house. Nicer places have come and gone with the years, but lingering among the remnants of boyhood, those spring moments on the cellar door loom large, giving a sense of shelter for colder winds of any day or any year.

How fascinating that the sun's warmth can penetrate so deeply or last so long. We are like trees after all. A mystic chlorophyl courses our mental veins to store in memory cell, if not in body cell, precious spring warmths against colder winters. This insight fortifies my will to abandon work. This now is no hedonistic escapade. I am working for my future, building, strengthening, re-inforcing. The final restraints pull free. I can enjoy the sun.

A feeling of nobility can rationalize almost anything.

Redbud Spring

*Beauty
    is nutrition
        for the inner self.*

Writing

I noticed almost from the start that in order to make any progress with writing, I had to remove from sight all irrelevant and extraneous notes and papers. Crossing out or laying aside wasn't enough. Just the knowledge that an unmanageable idea is written down on that piece of paper on the left corner of the desk is enough to paralyze my pencil and inhibit the free flow of thought. A decision is required. Throw it on the floor with the rest of the rejects or hide it among the other half-finished thought-starters, but don't—by proximity—let it influence current production.

Quite possibly this is why personal appearances are so important . . . why we conduct personal matters behind closed doors . . . why we decorate our environment . . . why we desire art . . . why manners and social convention are so important. The list is endless. We are working on the environment within which our lives are being written and an activity this important requires proper stimuli to produce proper results.

My obsession with external stimuli extends to the pencils I cradle in my hand, the way they glide over the paper and the sound they make as they do so. Paper doesn't seem to be an issue. I think, deep down, I take some pride in writing on "scrap paper" as if ideas come tumbling out so unexpectedly as to preclude having conventional paper around. It does happen—but it is hardly a formula. Clean, unobstructed paper, however, is a requirement for anything more than a word or phrase. Again, no external stimuli in the form of words, scribbles, ideas, can be tolerated unless specifically required by the task at hand—hence the rubble on the floor.

→

The simple, disciplined, purposeful life is so much to be admired. In the first month of college, I wrote a phrase for my guidance that I still possess: (the secret of life is) "singleness of mind and definiteness of purpose." Even though I wish I had followed my own advice more devoutly, I'm impressed that the insight came so early and stayed so long. The clutter of living has a way of steaming up the windows of our vision until we lose sight of the road ahead. Only decisive, purposeful activity—like cleaning out the refrigerator—can restore the vision.

By contrast, I love to work in the midst of clutter. Crumpled paper on the floor, papers, notes, books, tea cups, cookie crumbs, napkins, finished and unfinished work—all contribute to the atmosphere of "work in progress". I know by the clutter that my mind is in motion—that ideas are being born, nurtured, and finalized. Then—in the end—there is the one corrected final statement of my life, like one more page of living finished. For better or for worse, this is who I am. This is me.

The Side Door

Windstorms
　shake old birdnests
　out of trees.

A Rain-softened Quiet

A rain-softened quiet shrouds the trees and the grasses. From somewhere under the oak leaves a cricket chirps and down the lane a scarlet tanager sings brightly. Chickadees, too, and a wren, have begun to sprinkle the quiet with song.

A fox squirrel has found a pool of water in an empty flower tub and hangs downward into it to drink. Finished, he moves toward me, unaware of my presence. With an awkward, rocking waddle, he walks almost up to my feet, where he stands erect, paws folded, to study me. A bluejay call alerts him and he nervously edges away and out of sight.

Again, in the cedar by the studio, two bluejays scold raucously. A chipmunk dashes, tail up, across the dangerous open stretch he worries about. In this rain-blessed woods and fields, life picks up its pace.

It has calmed me. The thunder-rumblings at dawn only made the dry cozy bed all the more delectable. Perhaps some ancestral wisdom, born of the dry rain-starved prairies of my boyhood perceives the rain as a protector, staving off disaster for another day.

Whatever—the cool, oxygen-rich air is invigorating. Were it not for my need to see and hear every little move of life around me, I would enjoy working vigorously. The moment is too alive. I'm locked in its life-bubbling embrace. Everywhere new sounds, new activities, break forth. All the world has taken a shower and now settles back to enjoy.

Jewels of Dawn

*Our curiosities
are the diamonds
of our minds.*

First Journey

Dianna's Colt

However strong the urge to leave home, to declare an independence, the urge to return is equally as strong. We are bound to our origins by thoughts, by feelings, by memories. Because of them, we venture more securely into the unknown and the untried. From this umbilical cord of memory another home is fashioned . . . and another.

So the journey goes. Fortified by legends and by an abundance of "as my mother used to say . . . ," we change and grow, save and modify, explore and challenge . . . and continue.

Foxtail

*The things
 that make us real
 are free.*

Just Over the Ridge

Rendezvous at Dawn

A Scar Upon the Land

A house will be built here—because we wish and now because we must. We are committed. Processes once begun produce their own energy—often their own direction.

The enormity of it all overwhelms us. We feel like warriors girding for battle or pioneers loading Conestoga wagons on the edge of a hostile prairie. So much will change. Will the newness truly be of our own creation, or will unrelenting forces beyond our control design and build our new world? We breath deeply and determine firmly.

We stand on the knoll that is the house site realizing we shall be the last to feel the simple private beauty of this perspective. This winter three deer stood here to survey the emerging studio across the drive. We saw where they came out of the oaks to stop to mull over the changes in their world. Will they grace us with their presence again? How cleverly can we blend our habitation into what has been theirs since time began? Their acceptance seems so important to us now.

So much of human activity produces ugliness. Our thoughtlessness, our indifference, our laziness—all those negative sides of us—conspire to work a scar upon the land. Nature does what it can, covering our trash, blooming through our wasted technology—and given time—it always works. But we are always doing more. Bulldozer mentalities relentlessly assault the gentle earth. Vulgar, careless minds dump their refuse aimlessly.

This we will not do . . . cannot do . . . but we must begin with an incision on this knoll. So we make the physician's promise to make it whole again.

→

Beginnings

*Real danger
  lies not in the risk,
  but in the fear of it.*

It is the process that is most ugly. No matter how hard we try, getting there is messy. Holes must be dug, spaces cleared, dirt dumped unceremoniously somewhere. Not unlike adolescence (the formative years!), building is a cluttered, confusing time. Only the dream keeps it all alive and sensible. The working drawings carry the vision, and in the midst of it all we return to them as often for reassurance as for direction.

In the end, there must not be a scar upon the land. It is unconscionable to be less artistic than a Baltimore Oriole or even a mourning dove. Up on the ridge beside the old stone pile, a woodchuck has a home so blended into his surroundings as to be invisible to all except the seasoned woodchuck-watcher. That is artistry. True, his is for survival—but isn't ours also at stake? How can we survive while out of harmony with nature? Can we live long . . . if not pleasantly . . . in the midst of ugliness? Deadened sensibilities is perhaps a greater death than loss of breath.

No. It must fit—all that we do. The process will not be complete until then.

One of our temptations is to harden everything—our paths, our living spaces, our work spaces—even our lives—so we can live with the changes technology brings. So, along with cement and asphalt, we use harsh colors, hard music, brittle social relationships, quick food, gleaming metal—all directed toward our own survival in the world we think must be. Explain that to your new-born child . . . if you can. "You must become hard, my child, if you are to survive!" That, too, is a scar upon the land, and all scars are hard, no matter how inflicted.

Lest we forget, let us be reminded that all growing things are tender—most tender and vulnerable at their most actively growing point. As I try to build my life—not just upon this land, but among all that is—it is my growing edges that promise most: an un-formed idea . . . a plan for which I am soliciting courage . . . a relationship of trust just begun . . . a dream still shapeless . . . an emerging skill.

→

Whatever tomorrow will be, its design lies in one of these. "So be gentle with me, my friend, I am still becoming. I hurt and bruise easily."

So says the land to us. Some of the terrain upon which we must build is sandy, tending to arid. The growth upon it is hard won—sparse stubborn lichen and clumpy dune grass. The thin layer of leaf mold from the pin oaks and hickories will now be destroyed. Only our caring can replace it.

The studio is now in place. I miss the winding path up the ridge to the summer house. Another will have to emerge, but the building fits. Long, low sloping eaves hover over the slope, mothering the earth, grouse-like. Gentle browns of roof and wall blend quietly with oak and cedar. I can work here. I look out upon the land without guilt. This is not a scar upon the land. Next fall when the brown leaves of the oaks and the yellow of the aspen swirl to rest along the foundation, the healing will be complete.

And so, reassurred, we embark upon the process of the house. We will watch the deer adjust their lives and they will watch us adjust ours. To every inflicted injury we will bring our thoughtful healing. Like all injuries, this one will take time—and love—love most of all.

Spring Parade

*The inquiring mind
survives,
blossoms,
and, eventually,
bears fruit . . .*

Contemplation

The time spent in contemplation is the most important time of our lives. Whatever more we are than mere sensors or experiencers comes from those times. To see or experience something and not to understand its meaning is the cruelest form of poverty possible. Like a primate playing with treasures, the unreflective person never knows the wonder of it all.

*The difference
between ignorance
and knowledge . . .
is effort.*

My Morning Path

Nag's Head Morning

*No clever wash
can turn mediocrity
into art.*

Albuquerque Moonrise

After the Rain

After the rain, the world started over. All the marks of traffic were gone—tracks erased, dust washed away, finger prints of activity scrubbed clean. Droplets of rain-light glistened from leaf tips and blades of grass. Like summer decorations, the rain lifted life to a level of celebration. Birds now announced "a new year." Chipmunks scurried about. A woodchuck emerged to test the possibilities. All the world breathed clean, fresh, new.

From the studio overhang, dripping water metronomed a rhythm of newness. Rivulets coursed the driveway, tracing the way to the lake and beyond. Shafts of sunlight pierced the cedars and the oaks, patterning the water laden grasses beneath.

Since the dawn of time, the process has gone on. Turmoil and struggle leaving their marks on the daily scene . . . then rains coming to make things new again. Wilted leaves will rise erect, colors sparkle again, old animosities momentarily stilled.

It is easy here at the Cedars to see this. There are no machineries of technology to deny the cycle, endeavoring to create a level plane where all things go on routinely uninterrupted. On life's paved streets, the rain is a mere inconvenience, made obsolete by umbrella, roof and windshield wiper. Sidewalks deny the rain, forest paths do not. Paths here respond, becoming soft, sensuous, and alive to each imprinting footstep.

How much easier the rainy days of our personal lives would be if we could live with them as the natural world does with theirs. These days do come. No cleverness or determination on our part can avert them. They are part of the cycle of life and we are equipped for them. We have the capacity to cry, to grieve, to sorrow. Our body can throb with fear, or anxiety. Our skin grows cold, clammy with apprehension. Knees weaken, arms ache with loneliness. We are built to respond to the storm and to the rain. What is hard, is to accept them as the cleansing agents they are. This takes an act of intelligence, of thought, of reflection. It is an act of will and not easy by any standards.

→

Reflections in the Rain

The rainy days truly do cleanse our being, putting the rest of life into perspective—forcing us to halt the mad rush of destiny, to take time out, to accept our frailty. Delusions of power and omnipotence come easily in a world defined by instants of convenience, by guarantees of comfort and success. Without the "rains" to restore our perspective, we endeavor to be gods, raging when things do not go as we wish.

Strange how adversity feeds the psyche. Hardly a destroyer, adversity presents us times for building, for strengthening. When the years have gone by, these are the tales we recount with fondness and pride. Sunny days slip into less sharp focus. Rainy ones become landmarks that prove our worth.

Yes . . . sometimes the storm downs the tree—even the young and healthy tree. Nothing comes of denying the danger, the possibility of destruction. What is equally true is our fascination with the threats to our survival. We create our own "storms" to test or strengthen our lives. We run races, climb mountains, fight duels of wit and strength, explore the edge of the precipice, take the gamble, bet the horse race. Ultimately, for some, the confrontation of win or lose all becomes the pinnacle of achievement. It becomes a championship game where an entire life is tested for its validity or worth.

This rain was none of that. It came slowly, grew in intensity and softened gently into silence. Watching it was restful, restorative. Its sounds and odors peaceful, quieting.

The black clouds from which it came were threatening enough—rolling turbulently out of the west as they did. But thunder rumblings and electrical flashes tapered quickly into steady, refreshing downpour.

Only the apprehension, the expectation of danger, created threat out of this storm. The natural world rejoiced in it, hungered for it. Without it, life would wither. Perhaps because we can worry, changes sometimes assume threat levels they do not really possess. How much of what we call "reality" is self-induced! Birthed in our →

own psyche, some tragedies can be dissipated in the same way—by our own self-understanding.

    The rivulets in the driveway are gone, as are the sparkling droplets from the trees. Insect noises announce a drier world. Like the deep sighs with which we pronounce peace, this day now declares all is well. Life is good.

Queen Anne's Morning

Summer Evening

A Path Once Taken

Together

Anything we touch
with love —
will be better.

The Portage

One June, in Quebec, on a grueling portage between Kikwissi and Lac Sairs lakes, Eric and I encountered mother love in its finest hour. This was to be a "short-cut", saving twenty-plus miles of paddling, giving us some leisure at Kipawa before beginning the drive home.

A forest ranger had assured us, "We go that way all the time. It is a good portage." Since we already had two weeks of adventuring behind us, and, needing no more grueling work to make us woodsmen, we accepted his recommendation and his directions.

What he neglected to add was this: HIS journeys were in the winter time on a snowmobile. It WAS shorter—the way a drop over the cliff is shorter than safe meandering switch-backs to the valley below.

We entered the ordeal at 10:00 a.m. If it were not for the grouse, I would block the experience totally from my mind. It wasn't long as portages go—probably two-plus miles—and it began quite promisingly. Built as a winter logging route, the portage went directly with no nonsense from bay to bay. Now in mid-June, the trail was, at best, ankle-deep muck. At its worst, it was a granite-strewn rockslide, moss covered and devoid of any secure footing whatsoever. A rotted log bridge pretended its way over part of it. It seemed a better alternative, but only three tentative steps on it sent me to the rock slide itself. A canoe on my shoulders did not function well as a balance pole, so every slip promised a fall. At one point, my right leg plunged through a moss blanket hip-deep into the rocks. How I managed to stand upright again, only my stamina could explain.

Beyond this lay three small stagnant ponds—each requiring loading, paddling across, and unloading. Beyond these stretched a swamp that slowly deepened until it merged into a slender finger of water and then out into Lac Sairs. Five individual portages in all—and three trips for each—were required. Two trips each should have been enough, but here it wasn't.

→

Solitude

Love . . .
is the only truth
worth dying for.

The trail was overgrown—essentially unmarked. Beavers had added their own logging trails to the one we were trying to follow. Trial and error became our pathfinding method, taking us much of the time through dark, swampy forest passageways randomly lit by single shafts of sunlight.

. . . And there was no drinkable water . . . along the way—OR at either end. Accustomed as we were to quenching our thirst from alongside the canoe whenever we chose, this deprivation was the cruelest blow of all. Knee deep in water most of the time, we were without a drop to drink.

At the driest point of the crossing, we met the grouse. She was busily educating 4 or 5 chicks in the fine art of "following mother". Obviously hatched that morning, the chicks were absorbing things like "hide in the grass", "follow the leader", and "listen to mother", as best they could. They had not yet been taught enough about camouflage to satisfy mother, so our presence here set her into a dither. Torn between playing "decoy" for the chicks and supervising their proper movements, she vacilated between one and the other until all of us were thoroughly confused. We stood stock-still in our tracks. The chicks clustered together, avoiding water and obstacles. Mother was a gyroscope of activity. Paralyzed in our tracks, we hoped she would solve this somehow. Finally, her frenzy erupted into a violent attack on my right leg. It was the object nearest to her chicks and obviously the greatest danger to them. Eric was riveted slightly beyond.

Time and again she threw herself against this enemy a hundred times her size and totally unknown. In between attacks, she maneuvered her brood across the path towards our left, attacking time and again to ensure their safety. Even after they were safely on their way, our first move brought her back as ferociously loving as before. She was beautiful! If we could have embraced her, we would have done so.

No, I didn't photograph her or her brood. I know . . . I missed a
→

chance of a lifetime, but I've made it a solemn practice—I do not intrude on sacred moments. The imprint on my memory and my psyche would be more than record enough. Besides, who knows what vengeance this mother might have brought down upon us for THAT hostile intrusion!

She made the way lighter. On the return journey for the second load, we saw her again, and she exchanged threats with us. On the return from that trip, she was out of sight, hopefully prepared for whatever new monsters might cross her family's path.

For us, the thoughts of her family devotion dimmed the dark thoughts of vengeance we were planning for that Quebec ranger who promised us "an easy half-hour's trip".

Eight hours later, as the sun touched the tree-tops, exhausted beyond description, hungry, soaked and worried about a camp-site, we pushed the loaded canoe out into the lake, the ordeal behind us.

We tied up alongside a downed cedar in the shelter of a high granite cliff, and, on a small rock ledge, lit the primus stove to eat a meal fit for royalty. That it was a mediocre instant rice casserole mattered not. It was hot, tasty, and energy-giving . . . and we were safe.

Our talk consisted of two things—a camp-site and the grouse family. It seems now that the latter reassured us of the possibility of the first. Such love as we had witnessed made light of any problem we might encounter.

On the way to a place to sleep, we saw another mother—a mallard duck, this time—just as harried, but with another philosophy of child care. Her brood consisted of either 21 or 22 two-week-old ducklings. As we rounded an island, startling them into activity, she rose partially from the water and wing-walked over the surface in advance of her enormous brood. Their response was to imitate her exactly with 44 frothing foot-propellers in her wake. When they neared where she waited, the process began again. Tired or not, they frothed dutifully behind her. →

A meaningful journey is more to be desired than any destination.

We detoured out into the lake to diminish these repeated frenzies until mother and flock felt safe enough to glide into the shelter of shore-line brush to let us pass.

Surely they couldn't have all been her original hatch. Such prolific production would discourage further motherhood forever. Possibly her collection was the result of some disaster to another mother, though possibly we were witnessing a genuine Quebec duck-day-care-center.

As the evening twilight softened into dark, we found refuge at a remote fly-in camp and slept the sleep of wanderers home at last.

Love is the only truth worth dying for. Here on a miserable portage in Quebec, where our own existence had been mildly threatened, we encountered such love twice in one day.

This most necessary of all attributes is both the simplest and the most difficult to acquire. Like blood and oxygen, love must permeate our being if we are to be alive. Unlike blood, or oxygen, love must be implanted in our lives by learning and practice. It helps to have been loved. Those grouse chicks will have an excellent role model for living and loving. Once learned, however, loving also takes practice if it is to become part of our lives. The price we pay for superiority over the grouse or the mallard is the act of will necessary to become as noble as they. For my part, that act of will became a little bit easier because we portaged this "easy half-hour" journey that one day in Quebec in June.

Journey's End

Day's End

*When we want the best
 for others,
We will know the best
 for ourselves.*

The Gentle and the Firm

*Everyone
deserves excellence . . .
Only the disciplined
ever achieve it.*

Along a Lonely Stretch

Beachwalker

The Deep Dark Hole of the Night

In the pre-dawn darkness, life's very existence is challenged. Doubts assail the direction, the purpose, the accomplishments of all the days before. Outside the window, the cold, grey-black night, like the deep dark of mind and spirit, has defeated the hopes and dreams born of sunny days. If breathing were not automatic, it, too, would cease—a victim of the depressing darkness, internal and external.

For the deep dark hole of the night is matched by a gut-wrenching dread that perhaps I have reached for more than I could achieve . . . that the dream is beyond my grasp . . . stars in another nebula. Perhaps my ambitions were heights the gods would not allow, demanding humbler achievements, lesser dreams.

For in my darkness, all the world has passed me by. A dark dread that I have done it all wrong crowds out any temperate perspective. No achievement seems important. No earlier joy retains any glow of support. That others care, or that others need and want me is as hollow as the deep black hole of the night. I am depressed.

My mind parades through the "if only's" and the "what might have been's". I rework every mistake, dwelling on the critical moment when the damage was done, wondering why it happened and how it could have been prevented. Others never make mistakes like this. Only I am the failure, and the dawn will not be welcome, for in it I must—joyless—go to work against insurmountable odds and . . . I will lose.

"It is only a down cycle" . . . the words are vacuous cliche'. The night's reality precludes simplistic cures. Sleep is impossible. No →

escape is visible, yet in the depths of the dark, a tiredness finally overtakes mind and body. Sleep comes.

Years ago, in another life, I learned how to overcome the "darks". So simple, it almost was too hard to do, for terrible states should demand complex cures, should they not? The method? Do something for someone else . . . no matter how insignificant. Only when I was determined not to be brought out of the "darks" did this not work—for then I couldn't bring myself to employ the method . . . because I knew it would work!

This morning, activity again saves the day. All the dark times are inward-turning. Self-examination turns morbid. Worries magnify. Self-doubts strengthen. Weaknesses grow more dominant. The demon of fear inhabits our nights, beyond the redemption of the light.

As I write, the "darks" seem so unreal. The composite memory of 4:00 a.m. vigils cannot be challenged, but their power is gone. Outside, under the cedar, grey slate juncoes, cardinals, chickadees, and nuthatches feed continuously. Beyond the protective curtain of shrubs and trees I know that somewhere several deer browse and move about. Beyond here, at home and in other corners and other houses, I am loved, respected and cared for.

Here, too, at the Cedars, our dreams are generated and I look out at them. I am writing in the part of them that is complete and try to visualize the rest. The knowledge that in the process of achievement, every dream looks like work, gives perspective to the remaining portions of the dream.

Work redeems the incapacitation born of the dark. The very immobility of our "dark times" creates a helpless, defeated mood. Only the objectivity of reaching out, working, doing something for others can fill the "black hole of the night". We cannot outrun the demon of the dark, but we can incapacitate him. We must live in the presence of our enemies always, but we need not fear them.

It is not what we have done that gives life meaning. It is what we →

Loneliness reminds us . . . the struggle to care is worthwhile.

ARE doing. Here is the strength for the night or for the day. We are the product of all we have ever done or been. We are accumulation of days—a summary of living through strength and weakness. What haunts us now is our absence of naiveté. Being brave at 21 is not an achievement. Being brave at 45 or 65 is. Our very understanding of the frailty of life makes us vulnerable. We have been chastised by hollow victories and fruitless efforts. We have worked long and hard at something only to discover it was of lesser importance than we assumed.

Now, simpler things are more cherished. It is harder to endow meaningless activity with great significance. Age brings an honesty if it brings anything at all.

Outside, the leaves are falling. The days are growing colder. Greyness, dampness, are more the order of things. Strangely, this is comforting. Things do change. Life does in truth run in a cycle. Next spring, that female cardinal I am watching, if she survives the winter, (and I shall help . . .) will build a nest and sing the song of family again. The trick is simple . . . survive the winter.

The "deep dark hole of the night" is gone—from mind and spirit as well as from the sky. The catharsis of thought is complete. Tasks I want to do hurry my pen. I must leave the contemplative life and, as Tennyson said, "be up and doing, with a heart for any fate . . . still achieving, still pursuing . . . learn to labor and to wait."

Pain . . .

   is a catalyst

     of thought.

Nova Scotia Rocky Shore

*It is not our imperfections
 that destroy us . . .
It is our inability
 to rise above them.*

Gentle Morning

The longer rays of the September morning sun are slanting over the ridge, edging the dew-damp trees in gold. In this crisp, invigorating quietness, I am trying to assimilate the night's deprivations. Sometime during the darkened hours since I last was here at the studio, an ugliness had invaded our privacy, leaving calloused, indifferent tracks in the soft sand where they had taken away part of our lives.

The robbery had hurt and outraged—less because of the economic loss than because of the loss of serenity. That evil would come out of the dark to molest our tranquility had never occurred to me . . . the possibility, yes, but not the fact. Now it had come, and for that loss there was no insurance coverage possible.

Then it happened.

To my left, just beyond the first cedar, a fawn was approaching, nose up, testing the air to learn what I was. With such candor and innocence, she probed what I might be. Then she moved down the driveway, inspected the red flag by the well, and moved over into the clearing beyond. I cautiously scanned the area for the doe.

She came from behind the poplars, searching the horizon for dangers to her children—for as she appeared, so did another fawn. Twins—tawny, grey-tan—their disappearing spots showing only on their flanks. The doe shook her head, lifted a back leg to scratch the offending ear, nibbled at a poplar branch and a clump of grass at its base. She watched her children, surveyed her surroundings. That she was fifty feet away from the studio was of no concern. It had appeared here in her world as so many other things had.

Her morning was relaxed, serene. Life was good for this family. The twins nosed each other and nibbled casually at the clover along the drive. →

Then the doe saw me, locking her eyes on my presence. For longer than I cared to, I stared back, immobile as I could manage. When she looked back over her shoulder to check the area behind her, I tried to move. Her gaze flicked back to me, identifying me as a human being. Still casual, alert, she returned her attention to her children. They were still doing children-things. Back to me. I decided to be alive and I turned my head to better see the twins. Her head went up a notch, ears farther forward, studying me now more intently. Then caution took over and she moved to her left behind the junipers and beyond my vision.

The twins—like the children they were—left the danger-watching to mother, moving leisurely about, making their examinations of their world. Something startled the fawn closest to the drive and she shied abruptly. That was enough. From the shelter of the junipers, the doe snorted a warning, triggering the twins into immediate flight. My time together with the family was over.

The healing, however, was complete. Going down to the well, I looked for the twin-wedged shapes of the fawns' footprints—footprints more powerful in my life than those tennis-shoe disfigurements left by the evil of the night.

No, the tranquility was not gone, and never had been. Like the doe and her family, my world was, and is, full of uncertainty. She has no worries about thieves among her kind . . . such ugliness is a human creation . . . but her existence is always in doubt. How, in the face of the her dangers, she could project such peace and serenity was a restorative marvel. It would now be embarrassing for me as a thinking being to do less. She moved with caution but not in fear and when she called her children away, it was caution rather than fear that moved her to action.

In how many ways are we robbed! Raucous noise shatters our quiet. Speed, congestion and adolescent selfishness turn our highways into ribbons of torture. Ignorant, pushy advertising assaults our sensibilities. Greed, dishonesty destroys trust between friends. Conflict of wills, frustration, turn families into battlefields. →

Contentment is a luxury— not available to the dishonest.

Lies, pompous fakery make mockery of the electoral process . . . and on it goes . . . look for more and you will find it.

There is more to life than ugliness coming out of the night. There is gentleness and quietness . . . love and affection . . . trust and comradeship. As real as the violent, the gentle survives and sustains us. These may not dispel the "things that go 'bump' in the night", but they diminish and control the power of evil over us.

Walk bravely into the face of uncertainty. Let not fear create the future. Caution is wisdom . . . fear is not. Like all the natural world—the doe family and mine—no other way of facing the morning is workable. I must believe. I must trust. Like the sun, I must "rise and shine", or the darkness will be mine and it will remain forever.

Meadow Muse

Cattails

Art . . .
*   is a buffer zone*
*   against*
*   a colder world.*

South Manitou Light House

*Life is too short
to spend it
in the preservation
of mediocrity.*

Touch of Water Running

Silver Seas

*What we dare
    is more significant
    than what we fear.*

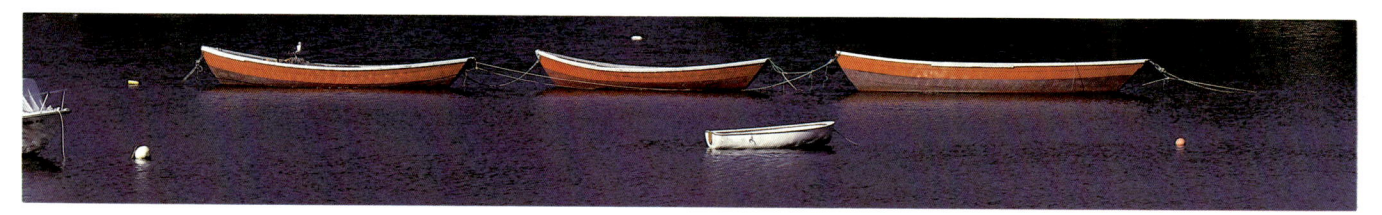

Three Red Boats

At the Water's Edge

Solitary sun-seekers, each making their own fragile journey into self, separated along the still, warm expanse of beach, allowing just enough space and silence to make their journey possible.

A Mourningcloak, having been lured from its cocoon security by the premature Spring warmth—and having silence and space of his own—fluttered along the water's edge. I followed in his wake, emulating the poetry of flight, the promise of lyrical abandonment . . . until he—possessing powers beyond mine—mounted a warming updraft to soar in magnificent crescendo over the rocks and into the woods beyond.

My spirit, alone, followed—reveling in that fragile freedom that makes all other journey's more tolerable.

Along the shore, I plied the established trade of all beachwalkers—pondering the stones underfoot, selecting those colors, those shapes, those textures I could not resist. These I carried until the wisdom of experience prompted me to return them to the rhythm of water, the cry of gull and child, and the crunch of another beachcomber's step.

→

This was a time for renewal and I stayed beyond the deadline my daily schedule imposed. Nature's time-table seemed a greater wisdom for today. This morning I could define freedom and wealth without the currency of commerce.

I knew once more what I truly wanted from life—and perhaps a little better how to achieve it. Here was a morning to provide more threads with which to weave the mantle of self-understanding necessary for colder, noisier days.

Some years ago, my son, playing on a similar beach, abruptly halted his beach business to hand me a triangular, smooth, brown stone with unforgettable words attached: "Here, this is for you . . . because I love you." Just as abruptly, he returned to his search of the beach.

Stone in hand, tears in eye, I watched him and gave thanks for his love—but more, for his ability TO love, and for his willingness to reveal it.

Today, remembering, I returned to my dropped stones and pocketed one of them, a stone not unlike that earlier stone in color and shape, a gift to myself on this warm, restorative Spring journey along the water's edge with the Mourningcloak. It will help keep me here in spirit, knowing as I do that this is freedom and this is wealth.

I still have the stone my son gave me 33 years ago, and he still the ability to know and to show love. I shall keep today's stone as well—more because of that earlier memory than anything else. If life is anything, it is love and the joy of loving. We can easily say, "It is only money . . .", but no possible circumstance could make us say, "It is only love . . ." That juxtaposition of concepts should establish beyond discussion the pre-eminence of love as the primary value in life.

Still, we need all the help we can garner if we are to nurture that essence. How fascinating that one small stone, properly anointed with words and feeling, can do so much.

No one is alone when they are respected.

Charlevoix Harbor

Beyond friendship,
  there is the knowledge
  that someone understands
  what we are all about
  . . . and cares.

Dune Crest

Fish Shanties

*Complexity
is dispelled
by the truth.*

The Orange Boat

Truth . . .
    makes a difference . . .
        only when we live by it.

Sable Island Boats

*Only those things
 that defy measurement,
 turn out in the end
 to have ultimate value.*

Life comes
  from what we are doing . . .
  more than
  from what we have done.

Fogbound

Dockside

*No risk is greater
than that
which bids us
settle for the least.*

A Leaf-strewn Path

Three Willow Leaves

Christmas

The Christmas of my boyhood memories will always be what Christmas was meant to be. In these memories, the tree is a fir tree, short-needled, spikey and gently tapered so that the candles, when lit, will not burn the branch above. One person, alone, will decorate that tree in the parlor behind closed doors on Christmas eve day. Its debut, then, will be after the evening meal—always lutefisk and lefsa . . . and if life has been bountiful . . . oyster stew. When the tree is lit for the first—and only—time, the "tree-trimmer" will open the parlor door and the family will come in to sit together in the darkened room while the candles burn down. As the last candle is extinguished, presents will be opened. This is the way it always will be.

There was a year or two of stockings hung on the oven door of the old cookstove. They never quite made it to a tradition because of my fourth Christmas. I still have a vivid memory of the handle of the red wagon stuffed awkwardly into the top of one of my own long stockings. Alongside the wagon lay two real snow-skiis. It seemed such a pathetic gesture. Santa Claus was supposed to put presents IN the stocking, not haphazardly attached to it . . . or so the story goes. The whole thing looked to my four-year-old perspective like something my father would do—especially since I had seen this wagon and those skiis under the branches of the two big fir trees outside the south-east corner of the house. Santa Claus never really got a good foot-hold in our house. My parents never were one to carry on a charade when the real thing was better.

Each of us had a special role in the celebration. My father caught, killed, and dressed the goose or the turkey for the Christmas Day meal. He built the tree stand and erected the tree carefully and securely. A tipped tree during the candle-burning could destroy the house.

→

As soon as I could carry wood or pull the other end of a cross-cut saw, it was my father's and my chore to collect the wood for the wood stoves in the kitchen and the dining room—and this week—in the parlor for Christmas eve and day. The kitchen stove this season required a very special kind of wood for the lefsa baking. The lefsa was baked on top of the vigorously-cleaned kitchen stove. The fire must be a hot . . . and an even, steady heat. My mother's reputation as a lefsa-baker was at stake and she supervised every load I carried in to dump into the kitchen wood box. Cutting these slender sticks of hardwood—ash, mostly—was tricky and my left index-finger bears a scar where once I was careless. In this most vivid memory of Christmas, my mother always wears an apron—a full wrap-around, pocketed apron—and a wisp of hair falls down over her face with a smudge of flour gracing her forehead where she has tried to brush it back. She always stands by the stove or the cupboard and she is always checking something in the warming oven above the stove. Occasionally she sings a bit . . . and always she is asking for more wood or water from the well. Not that I want to ever, but I cannot get very far away from the kitchen. Life centers here.

Our Christmas traditions were born mostly out of our lack of money. None of us thought of ourselves as poor. We just didn't have much money. So one of our Christmas traditions was that each person got one big gift from the other two. There were smaller gifts, too, as we were able to do—mostly clothes and other necessities. But it was THE gift that we got from the other two that made Christmas. Long before the season came, we were planning and scheming. No one EVER asked, "What do you want?". It must be a total surprise, and very special. What fun to scheme and plan! Then, close to Christmas, the guessing began. It was obligatory for each of us to guess what the others had gotten them . . . but equally obligatory to never find out. So most of the guessing was about where the present was hidden, not what is was. That way, →

even if you found out, the surprise was still alive.

I only blundered once—the Christmas I was thirteen. These were very difficult years and even one present was sacrifice. We were playing the guessing game after radio program was over and my mother was guessing. My father and I had gotten her a fountain pen—an Estherbrook pen. We were so delighted over our gift, for not only was she the letter-writer or the family, but her name was Esther. It was a perfect gift and we had a perfect hiding place . . . in the cow barn, safely on a ledge out of sight.

I was boldly challenging her to try to guess the hiding place when she said in playful resignation, "I bet you hid it in the cow barn!". I, in my adolescent eagerness, replied glibly, "O no, if we did, the cows would be writing all over the walls with it!". My father guffawed and I stared at him in disbelief that I had uttered the words. Then with priceless aplomb, my mother replied, "Well, if it is not there, then it must be in the attic." No matter what, the love of the game and the love for each other decreed a higher ethic than that of winning. Christmas eve, my mother was ecstatic over her surprise gift.

Other memories persist but never dominate. There was the get-to-gether on Christmas day for family or for neighbors to feast and share our gifts. There was sledding such as the flat prairie would allow and later there were trips to other places and other families. Perhaps privation bestows a preciousness to any celebration not available to the more affluent experiences. Perhaps Christmas, is, and always has been, a childhood creation. Whatever, Christmas, for me, will always be celebrated this way by three people in an old and often cold farmhouse on the South Dakota prairie.

Daybreak

*Polish
cannot make
an apple.*

Reflective Mood

Even in the pre-awakening moments, I was beset with quiet, reflective, probing thoughts that pre-empted the pretenses and the anxieties dawn often brings. What induced this analytical mood, I don't know. I awakened to it. Through all the morning's careful routines the attitude persisted—even now it moves my pen across this scrap of paper.

It is a private, golden, dawn-ish feeling—well beyond the touch of glitter and chit chat. I am real. My self-worth clearly intact with no price quoted on me or my production. Let the machineries of commerce pass me by. Today—this moment—I am me.

In this private, temporary, simplification of life I remember others whose lives seemed more like this always than I could manage . . . my mother's simple rock-hard faith in the goodness of life no matter how scarce the evidence of it . . . Herb May's scholarly committment to thought, study, truth . . . Carl Poe's indomitable joy of life and belief in people. Inwardly I know they were not like this always. Outwardly, my memory of them has preserved a simplified montage that makes them lodestones for thought and feeling. These are the jewels of my personal kingdom, the value standard on which the currency of my life is based. There are so many . . . Walton Cole, who helped me learn how to love my fellow man . . . my father who taught me how to work . . . Hugh Mather, whose incisive mind made it easier to know and to speak the truth.

→

There are the negative ones, too, scattered along the way like remnant wrecks of past ugly battles, but this morning they have no power. Good, alone, presides. This knowledge is in itself another victory over those dogged enemies of the past. Inwardly, I can almost giggle . . . I am secured by this contemplative mood that simplifies things until their primary strength is all-prevading and dominant . . I am me—alone and secure.

The passage of time makes all this possible, I know. There are contemporary giants whose lives could be—or are—lodestones as well. But like new wine, they have not aged in the cellars of my mind long enough to command the respect that time will give them. Memory is the fabricator of heroes—memory and desire. This does not deter me. I know I need my heroes. I am unabashed by this child-like pursuit. Too much of what we call "maturity" or "sophistication" is unworthy of the child's honesty. Innocence is not weakness. Cunning, force, deceit, power erode the inner self so that we cannot survive without the hard-shell armor of noise, glitter or narcotic sedation. When all that is really wanted is an ideal, the strength to follow it, and a hero to personify it.

Believing in people and in a person is a joyous experience, an act so enriching that little else is needed for the sustenance of life. And it all begins with the belief in "me" birthed as it was today in the pre-dawn yearnings of my subconscious.

The reflective mood is passing, but its strength remains, girding me for the "battle" most days present. Like solid, comfortable shoes, this mood has dressed me well for the day.

Like a tree —
we grow . . .
up and out
to embrace
the earth,
the sun,
the sky,
the wind.

Trillium

*Until we learn
 to respect the ordinary,
 the extra-ordinary
 escapes us.*

Hollyhocks

Truth . . .
  is not created by the way
  we put words together.

This Cloak of Mine

This cloak of mine, woven to protect and warm,
has yet another tear—a jagged, hurtful hole—
where once the vibrant threads of friendship
wove strength and love about my heart.

Now, piercing shafts of cold reach in to chill
where she, of fireside warmth and herculean strength,
once smiled against the years and held my hand
and led, when she was needed, to light the way.

No threads there are to weave or mend
a fabric such as hers, embracing threads
of warmth and strength, none can make again.
She was as breath . . . and blood . . . and life . . . and gone.

An impotent universe it is
that cannot save such wealth
and leaves instead a lonely spot—
a jagged void where once she laughed.

Some lives there are that should be saved
for reference points to chart the stars.
How can we find our way if all the best
is torn from our sight to burrow underground?

My cloak—now of many jagged holes—
still protects and warms, for in my heart
still lives the strength of those I've loved,
and here, no ravages of time can rob or tear.

Never quite enough—as enough is measured—
but who will quibble, when this is all?
Better than none at all, a voice in memory
is often voice enough to call us out of pain.

A laugh, a gesture, a presence, a fleeting vision,
does so much more than we dream possible—
mending as they do those jagged holes
torn in the sheltering cloak of our life.

Gone, the person, the living presence of a friend.
But close the eyes, does she not yet live?

      And so . . .

I take my pen and magic paper and write,
to tell her once again that she is loved and needed yet.

Two Tulips

Dogwood

Jason's Bucket

Blueberry Summer

The Yellow Tufts of Summer

Leelanau House

Yellow Tufts of Summer

The yellow of the goldenrod has gone from the ridge and the slopes to the west. Now white-tufted seed pods wave gently in the west wind that slips up the slope to riffle the hawthornes in front of me. This going and coming surprised me a bit. Perhaps I expected the yellow glow on the hillside to stay forever—not that I wanted it to. I have no abiding love for goldenrod.

Change is like that. Much as we know it will come, its appearance jars us in our complacency and we have to move our mind-clock ahead to the present.

I wonder about the aging process in myself. Has my "yellow glow" yielded to the "white tufts" of age? How will I know? Nature gives its clues surely, else who will tell me? My age? It is a numerical incident . . . fifty-five and over . . . senior citizen discount? Perhaps my body, slowing down from a more frantic pace, will tell me.

Numbers seldom tell all. I taught adolescents far more "aged" than I. Their boredom, their disinterest, their indolence, their cynicism, eminently qualified them for a room beside the most senile. By contrast, when I was thirty-five, my most interesting conversationalist was Walter Pielmeier—then ninety years on the numerical scale.

No, the numbers are wrong. Goldenrod doesn't say, "Oh, I've blossomed for 30 days now, its's time to go to seed!" Other forces tell it that.

Love of life and its enthusiasms is a quality of the mind. We are as young as we are in mind and spirit. The exterior is our handicap, not our source. Even in the white tufts waving in this September wind, next year's yellow glow lies waiting. Each of us is the same boy, the same girl, we always have been. Nothing can change that. How nice!

→

So, if we have retired, as we all shall, let it not be from life. That ominous word—retire—literally means "to withdraw from the scene." How frightening! How wrong!

How familiar . . . At twelve, I had to prove my age did not prevent me from driving a tractor. At nineteen, it was to make my own decisions. At thirty, that I was old enough to get the job . . . at fifty, that I wasn't TOO old! On it goes. . . .

At every age our physical, verbal, mental swords are as unsheathed as they ever were. About us always are dragons to slay, mountains to climb, rivers to run, meadows to peruse, ideas to explore. Here at the Cedars, where we live, there is more to see, more to experience, than time allows. Is this the scene from which I am to withdraw? How?

I ponder the dilemma, and in the lingering, life wells up to invalidate the body's numbers. As I sit writing, my mind and pen travel over the years without prejudice. Next year, I will have another to peruse and use—not better than any other, or less—but another gift to use as well as I can.

The time that I have stolen to write this, came from the work I must do as an artist. Living life goes on for all of us. I must be an artist if I am to live, and I must think and write if living is to have meaning. Nowhere does life itself become a thing of numbers.

The white tufts of the goldenrod declare it is time to reflect, to plan, to set the stage for next year's blooming. So that is what I do.

We do have our predators . . .
but, being more sophisticated,
they consume our minds
instead of our bodies.

Autumn Shadows

*It takes more
than arrogance . . .
to make excellence.*

Morning Watch

Dawn at Blue Rocks

*Only the journey
can make
the destination
worth while.*